A COMPLETE GUIDE TO
BODHGAYA
LAND OF ENLIGHTENMENT

J.P. Sharma

Invincible Publication Pvt. Ltd.

Published By

Invincible Publication Pvt. Ltd.

For permissions, contact:

Invincible Publication Pvt. Ltd.

1103-A, 11th Floor, SAS Tower, Sector 38, Gurugram Haryana- 122003

Phone: +91-124-4034247

www.invinciblepublishers.com

Sales Office: -4760-61/23, Basement, Pratap Street,

Ansari Road, Daryaganj, New Delhi - 110002

Email: invinciblepublishers@gmail.com

Title: A Complete Guide to Bodhgaya Land of Enlightenment

Author: J.P. Sharma

ISBN: 978-93-88333-08-5

This is a work of nonfiction. Every effort has been made to accurately represent the events and individuals featured. In cases where names or identifying details have been changed, it has been done to protect the privacy of individuals.

Printed in India

First Edition: 2018

Reprint: 2025

Buddha in Mahabodhi temple Bodhagayaa

ACKNOWLEDGEMENT

It is wanderlust which takes me from place to place. The endeavour to know Buddha and Buddhism inspired me to come to the places associated with his life and the places where he performed miracles. In his last days, Buddha says to Ananda that a follower of the faith should visit these four places at least once in his lifetime - Lumbini, his birth place; Bodhgaya, where he was enlightened; Sarnath, where he delivered his first sermon; and Kusinara, where he attains Nirvana. For more than three decades, Dhamma has been calling me from time to time to these places.

Inspired to the core of my heart in 2016, I got a book published on the journey of Buddha, 'Foot Prints of Gautam Buddha' covering all the places related to Buddha. Millions of people of faith and alike visit Bodhgaya, and because of a paucity of an authentic account, I dreamed a book on Bodhgaya, and here it is now 'Bodhgaya - Land of Enlightenment' in your hands. To gather information, I visited Bodhgaya many times, collected information and captured images in my DSLR. It being a dream come true, I wish to thank people who not only helped but also inspired me, Sri Kiran Lama - Secretary at Daijokyo monastery, Wenjia - a Chinese visitor and guest at the Chinese Buddha monastery, Acharya Nipun -Secretary at the Royal Thai monastery, Dr. Kalyan Priya - Abbot at the Bangladesh monastery, Sri N. Dorjee - Hon. Secretary at Bodhgaya Temple Management Committee, Ven P. Sheewalee Thero - Secretary Mahabodhi Society of India, Sri Mahendra Singh - retired Special Secretary Govt of U.P. and Vice President and Trustee, Mahabodhi Society of India, my friend Chandra Mohan Misra who accompanied me to the many places, my friend and photo critic Subir Roy, ex-photojournalist at The Hindu, and last but not the least, my wife Urmila Sharma, who not only allowed me to travel often alone but managed all home affairs in my absence.

INTRODUCTION

Siddhartha, the royal prince, meditated deeper and deeper under a Bodhi tree (pipal tree) in Uruvella on a full moon, and realised that he knew the truth. He understood why the world was full of suffering and unhappiness and how mankind could overcome those miseries of life two thousand and five hundred years ago. He had found the cause of sorrow and became enlightened - a Buddha.

According to the traditions of those days, his mother Mahamaya Devi was going to Devdaha, the home of her parents in Koliya Kingdom, to deliver her child. When Mahamaya entered the forest of Lumbini in the Tarai region of Nepal, trees of the forest bowed down to her in welcome and said, 'Enjoy this lovely garden of angles.' Queen Mahamaya Devi halted in Lumbini garden, walked around and eventually by holding the branch of a tree, gave birth to the holy child named Siddhartha, meaning the one who has fulfilled the purpose.

Mahamaya Devi had a dream before the birth of prince Siddhartha that a white elephant holding a lotus was entering her womb. Royal soothsayers predicted that the newly born child would either be the universal monarch or the enlightened one; 'Chakravartin' or 'Buddha'. Sage Asita visited Kapilvastu after the birth of this child. He laughed and shed tears upon seeing him. When asked the reason, the sage replied that he had laughed because the child would become a saviour, and shed tears because he would be no more to see this. Prince Siddhartha's mother died just 7 days after his birth, and he was brought up by his maternal aunt Prajapati Gautami.

Historians believe that Buddha was born in 563 or 566 B.C. and died (attained nirvana) in 483 or 486 B.C. Therefore, he lived during 5th and 6th century B.C. which was the period of great intellectual movement in the world. Confucius and Lao-Tse in China, Zoroaster in Iran, and Mahavira in India were contemporaries of Lord Buddha. During this period, there existed many developed cities in India like Magadha, Vaishali, Kapilvastu, Avanti, Kalinga, Videh Ang, Kasi and Pava, which were all well managed states.

Utmost care was taken in the upbringing of Prince Siddhartha. All worldly pleasures were provided to the royal prince. Prince Siddhartha was married to a beautiful princess Yashodhara (Bhadra Kapalayani) of Koliya king. A son was born to them and was named Rahul, as Siddhartha considered his son an obstacle in his spiritual path. Inspite of all materialistic pleasures, the sights of an aged man, disease, and death made him realise the futility of the materialistic world. One night, leaving his wife Yashodhara and Rahul asleep, prince Siddhartha embarked upon the search for knowledge.

After leaving home, Siddhartha practised austerities for about six years. Alar Kalam and Udrak Ramputra were unable to quench the spiritual thirst of Siddharth. As a result of practicing austerities, Siddhartha's body became weak and turned into a mere skeleton. He soon realised that this was not the right path. One day while meditating, he heard a song being sung by the women folk of the village. The song conveyed the message that do not tighten the strings of Veena (a musical instrument) so much that they break away, and do not loosen the strings so much that it cannot produce any music.

Siddhartha realised that the middle path (madhya marg) is the right path. He decided to have food. His five disciples thought that Siddhartha had chosen the wrong path, therefore they left him. He ate sweet rice cooked in milk (Kheer) given to him by Sujata, a village woman. In some scriptures, it is mentioned that the Gods mixed amrit (elixir) in it. On a full moon night during Vaishakha (a month according to the Hindu calendar), Siddhartha attained wisdom (Bodhi) and became Buddha. At some places, it is called Sambodhi. After attaining enlightenment at Bodhgaya, Buddha decided to preach Dhamma to his five erstwhile companions who had left him. Therefore, Buddha came to Sarnath near Kasi (present day Varanasi) and preached Dhamma for the first time. This event in Buddhism is called Dharmachakra Pravartan (turning the wheel of law).

During this time, the Vedas held supreme power in the religious domain and Brahmins were the sole custodians of religious activities. Caste system had also become quite deep rooted in the society by this time. Vedic rituals and animal sacrifices became an important part of the religion. In this religious atmosphere, Gautam Buddha preached a new path of salvation, which was very simple. He preached the Four Noble Truths of Arya Satya (Chatushatya): This world is full of miseries (Dukkha); Its cause is attachment (Samudaya); and by suppression (Nirodha) of all these attachments, Nirvana can be attained. Buddha preached the eight fold noble path (Arya Astangika Marg) called the middle path (Madhyam Marg), i.e. right view, right intention, right speech, right actions, right livelihood, right awareness, right mediation and right contemplation.
Buddha did not attach any importance to the matter of God or the soul because they were beyond the ken of human intellect. If a man desires to achieve a goal, he is cautioned to avoid involvement in complex and intricate matters concerning God and the soul. The moment he entangles himself, he is liable to forget his own self without solving his problem. Buddha's approach to human liberation was unique in its own way and differed radically from all philosophical approaches or religious thoughts that came before him. Buddha travelled to the then existing kingdoms of Kosala and Magadha i.e. Sarnath, Rajgir, Nalanda, Kausambi, Shravasti, Sankisa, Kapilvastu, Vaishali and Kusinagar (situated in the present day provinces of Uttar Pradesh and Bihar of the Indian Union) and spread his teachings. After the demise of Buddha, Buddhism remained dormant for more than two centuries.

In the war of Kalinga, the sight of thousands of human beings killed left a deep impression on the mind of King Asoka. Saddened by the tragic death of so many, Asoka embraced Buddhism and abandoned the means of war for the expansion of his kingdom. Instead, he adopted the policy of Dhammavijaya - the victory of religion. As a result of royal patronage thus, Buddhism not only flourished in India, but also reached the far boundaries of Sri Lanka. Asoka visited the holy Buddhist sites and erected stone pillars there. He built stupas at Sarnath, Kausambi, Lumbini, Bodhgaya and Vaishali which exist even today as testimony of his faith.

Satvahanas in the south, though followers of Brahminical faith themselves, were tolerant of Buddhism and gave impetus to it. During the reign of Satvahanas, Nagarjuna was a contemporary of Yagyasri Gautmi. Nagarjuna was a great Buddhist philosopher and exponent of Buddhism in south India. The place of his rule has been identified as Nagarjunakonda in the district of Guntur. Nagarjunakonda is about 160km from Hyderabad. A large number of Buddhist sites got submerged inside Nagarjuna sagar. Nagarjuna spent many years at Nalanda University. Many scriptures written by him are still available, while a translation of 20 scriptures into Chinese have been preserved. Only two scriptures of Nagarajuna, Madhayamik Karka and Vigrah Vyavaritini, are available in Sanskrit. In a man-made lake Nagarjuna sagar, a museum has been erected in and a transplanted site has been developed on the east bank of the reservoir where a few monuments have been reconstituted.

With the rise of the Kushana dynasty in India, Buddhism entered a new phase. Kanishka gave patronage to Buddhism. During his time, Buddhism reached China and Central Asia. Gupta rulers were worshippers of Vishnu, but during the Gupta period, the art and architecture of Buddhist monuments attained new heights. Gupta rulers patronised Nalanda University which was a great centre for Buddhist teachings. Chinese traveller Fa-hein visited Nalanda University in 409 A.D. during the Gupta period, while Hiuen-tsang visited in 637 A.D.; during the reign of Harshavardhan. Both the travelers have given glorious accounts of Buddhism in India. Traces of Buddhism are available all the way up to 1100 A.D. during the rule of a Pala King from eastern India. During the rule of the Pala king, Vikramsila University (situated in the present day district of Bhagalpur in the state of Bihar) was a great centre for Buddhist teachings. These world famous centres of Buddhist learning were annihilated and the holy books and manuscript were all burnt by a Muslim invader Bakhtiar Khilzi in 1235 A.D. - 1236 A.D.

Teachings of Buddha are preserved in the Tripitakas in Pali, namely: Suttapitak, Vinayapitak and Abhidhammapitak. These Pali tripitakas were not created at the same time or the same place. Pitakas were written at different times and at different places. Pali was the language of the Magadha Empire and Buddha preached his sermons in Pali, thus it is regarded as Buddha Vachan, authentic from the mouth of Buddha.

Just 3 months after the nirvana of Buddha, a dispute arose amongst the bhikshus regarding dhamma and vinay. To address the dispute, the first council (sangit) was organised in Rajgrah. The second council was organised a hundred years later in Vaishali, wherein some dispute relating to vinay was resolved. The third council was organised in Patliputra during the period of Asoka, and the Pali Tripitak were finalised in this council. The Pali Tripitak found today are the same which were given their final shape during the reign of Asoka. After the third council, Asoka sent his son Mahendra and his daughter Sanghmitra to Sri Lanka to propagate Buddhism. The fourth council was held during the reign of Kanishka in Kashmir. Since the period of Asoka, the two sects - Hinyan and Mahayan arose in Buddhism.

With the course of time, Buddhism reached beyond the shores of India to Nepal, Sri Lanka, China, Japan, Thailand, Korea, Burma, Cambodia, Laos and Bhutan, and is now followed by millions. According to Albert Einstein, "If there is any religion that would cope with modern scientific needs, it would be Buddhism."

Young Monk circumambulating Maha Bodhi Temple

MAHABODHI TEMPLE

Saddened to the core of his heart by the sight of an old man, a diseased man and a corpse being taken by mourners, Siddhartha left the luxuries of a princely life, while his wife Yashodhara and son Rahul were still asleep. Chana and his favorite horse Kanthak accompanied him upto the boundary of the Sakya Kingdom. After crossing the river Anoma which marked the boundary of the Sakya clan, Siddhartha cut away his locks with his own sword and handed over his royal robes and ornaments to Chana with the instruction to return to Kapilvastu. His favourite horse Kanthak could not bear to part from his master, and fell down to his death right there. Crossing over the countryside, Siddhartha reached the banks of Niranjana. Finding serenity in that place, Siddhartha decided to stay here. Because Siddhartha attained Bodhi (enlightenment) here, this place took on the name of Bodhgaya.Situated in the Gaya district of Bihar, a state of India, Bodhgaya is one of the holiest places for Buddhists world over. Siddhartha practiced austerities and penance for about 6 years in Uruvela on the banks of the river Niranjana (present name Phalgu). In the month of Vaishakh (a month according to the Hindu calendar), on a full moon night (Poornima), under the pipal tree (botanical name ficus religosa), in Buddhist texts, it is popularly known as Bodhi tree, Siddhartha attained enlightenment (Bodhi) and became Buddha.

Gate to Maha Bodhi Temple

Entrance to Maha Bodhi Temple

Asoka visited Bodhgaya and built the Vajrasan, a railing around the Bodhi tree and a pillar with an elephant on top. Alexander Cunningham was also of the opinion that the present Mahabodhi temple exists over the remnants of the Asokan structure. The Mahabodhi temple dates back to 2nd century B.C., which is evident from the remains found at the site. Promenade (Chankam) is also considered an early structure.

After attaining enlightenment, Buddha walked up and down this platform. It represents the lotus flowers which blossomed at his footsteps. Chinese traveller Fei-Huen who visited Bodhgaya in 409 A.D., has described three monasteries in his writings. Hiuen-Tsang visited this place after a lapse of two centuries in 637 A.D. and has described the construction of this temple to Asoka. Mahabodhi temple had early connections with Sri Lanka. A Buddhist from Sri Lanka made contributions for the construction of a boundary wall around the Bodhi tree. Some Buddhists visited Bodhgaya in 5th century A.D. The Pala kings of east India contributed to the repair of the temple. In thirteenth century, Burmese people also participated in the repair of the temple.

Mahabodhi temple escaped the atrocities of Muslim invaders. The temple is 170 feet in height with a 50 feet wide base and has the structure of a straight pyramidal tower. All four sides of the temple have several tiers of niches, while the front face has a lancet opening for light. The present day structure of the Mahabodhi temple is the result of numerous restoration activities carried over time. When this author visited Bodhgaya three decades ago, restoration work was being carried out at Mahabodhi temple, and he witnessed the same being carried out in 2018 too.

BODHI TREE

Bodhi Tree

Enlightened on a full moon night during Vaishakh, Buddha spent the first week under the Bodhi tree (Pipal, botanical name: ficus religosa). It is present on the west side towards the back of the present day Mahabodhi temple. The original tree under which Siddharth attained Bodhi has fallen several times. A twig of the original tree was carried to Anuradhapur in Sri Lanka. Alexander Cunningham planted saplings of the same tree at Bodhgaya in 1876 and the present tree has its origins in Sri Lanka.

VAJRASAN

Vajrasan

It is situated on the back side of the Mahabodhi temple, beneath the Bodhi tree. It is built out of chunar sandstone. It has length of seven and a half feet and has a width of four feet and three inches.

When the author visited Bodhgaya in 1993, there was no stone railing around the vajrasana. A stone railing was erected in the later years to protect the vajrasan and the Bodhi tree.

ANIMESH LOCHAN

Animesh Lochan

Buddha spent the second week at this spot. He gazed at the Bodhi tree without blinking his eyes, which gave this place the name Animeshlochan. This spot is towards the northern side of the temple. When a visitor enters the temple complex, this spot exists on the right hand side. Bodhgaya Temple Management Committee has erected here a temple similar to the main temple, but smaller in size.

CHANKRAMAN

Chankraman

Buddha spent the third week at this spot, meditatively walking up and down. This is a brick platform on the north side of the main temple. Lotus flowers are carved out on the platform to signify the lotus flowers that blossomed under the footsteps of Buddha. Chankraman is 53 feet long, 3 feet and 6 inches broad, and about 3 feet in height. In the early days, it was covered under a roof, but only the pillars remain now.

RATANGRAHA

Buddha spent his fourth week at this spot. It is a roofless structure to the northwest of the Mahabodhi temple. Buddha spent the third week in meditation here.

Ratangraha

AJPALA NIGRODHA TREE

Ajpala Nigrodha Tree

Buddha spent the 5th week at this spot. Just to the right of the temple entrance, there existed a tree where Sujata, daughter of the village headman, offered kheer (sweet rice cooked in milk) to Buddha.

MUCHLIND LAKE

Muchlind Lake

Buddha spent the 6th week here, near Muchlind lake. Near this lake is the Asokan pillar with a broken top. While Buddha was in meditation, Mara tried to disturb him with storm and rain.

The serpent king Muchlind then appeared and coiled around the body of Buddha and sheltered him with his hood. Buddha remained seated without any disturbance.

RAJAT TREE

Buddha spent the 7th and last week here under this tree. Since attaining enlightenment, Buddha met two merchant of Utkal, Bhall and Tapasu, here for the first time. Bhall and Tapasu became the first disciples of Buddha. In the last week, Buddha decided to propagate his wisdom for the benefit of mankind. From here, Buddha travelled to Kasi to initiate the Dhammachakra at Sarnath.

Being one of the most holy places in the world, millions of people, whether Buddhist or non-Buddhist, travel to Bodhgaya from across the globe to offer gratitude to Buddha. People who follow Buddhism were so impressed with this place, that they erected many monasteries in the architecture of their countries in Bodhgaya over a course of time. In every nook and corner of Bodhgaya, one can find a monastery.

Rajat Tree

SUJATA GARH

A brick stupa was erected to commemorate the residence of Sujata who offered kheer (sweet rice cooked in milk) to Buddha in Uruvela. The Archaeological Survey of India excavated this site in 1973-1974 and then again in 2001-06. They found a double terra-coated circular stupa with ayakas in the cardinal directions. The stupa was constructed in three phases from the Gupta period to the Pala period. Some of the antiques unearthed during these excavations are kept and displayed in the museum at Bodhgaya.

About 2 kms from Sujata Garh, statues of Sujata and Buddha are kept on a mound under a banyan tree (botanical name: ficus benglanisis). This place is called Sujata temple. Adjacent to it is a Shiva temple. All of these are modern structures and no archaeological remains have been reported from this place.

Sujata Stupa

Devotees at Sujata Stupa

A man holding umbrella to provide shade to Monk

MAHABODHI SOCIETY OF INDIA

Angarik Dharampal

Angarik Dharampal visited Bodhgaya on 22nd January, 1891. Looking at the depleted condition of the Mahabodhi temple, he decided to bring back its glory. What he felt is written in his diary in these words:
"As soon as I touched with my forehead the Vajrasana (the Diamond Seat), a sudden impulse came to my mind. It prompted me to stop here and take care of the sacred spot, so scared that nothing in this world is equal to this place where prince Sakyasingha gained enlightenment under the Bodhi tree."

The Bodh Gaya Mahabodhi Society was constituted at Colombo on May 31st 1891 with an object of establishing a Buddhist Monastery and college at Bodhgaya, representing the Buddhist countries of China, Japan, Cambodia, Burma, Ceylon, Nepal and Tibet. The name of Bodh Gaya Society was changed on 6th December 1915 to Maha Bodhi Society. Maha Bodhi Society was registered in Kolkata, where its head office was also established. In 1991, this society was named as the Maha Bodhi Society of India. Angarik Dharampal undertook the work of reviving Buddhism in India at Bodhgaya and Sarnath. A beautiful monastery has been erected in Bodhgaya at a distance of a few hundred meters from the Mahabodhi temple. A beautiful statue of Buddha has also been placed in one of the halls of the building. This building caters to the needs of Buddhist pilgrims from Sri Lanka and other countries as well.

Maha Bodhi Society of India

Statue of Lord Buddha in MBSI

ROYAL THAI TEMPLE

The Royal Thai Temple is erected in Thai architecture. The Government of Bihar provided land from the village Masti of Bodhgaya for this temple. A lease agreement between the Collector of Gaya and B. Chareonchai, a representative of the Royal Government of Thailand, was signed on 12th April 1958, vide which 4.57 acres of land was handed over to them from the 1st of May 1958 for a period of 99 years on an annual rent of Rs. 584. A large sized statue of lord Buddha and the beautiful decorations inside the temple give a peaceful ambiance to the visitors.

There are many other temples built by Thai people. Mettrama Buddha temple situated on the Bodhgaya–Gaya bypass road is built in white colour, which is another beautiful example of Thai architecture. On the Bodhgaya-Gaya bypass road, two other temples are under construction by the people of Thailand.

Royal Thai Temple

Royal Thai Temple

Statue of Lord Buddha in Royal Thai Temple

Mettarama Thai Temple Bodhgaya-Gaya Bypass Road

Thai Temple Bodhgaya Bypass Road

CHINESE MONASTERY

Chinese Buddhist temple is located barely a few hundred meters away from Mahabodhi Temple. It was founded by TanYunshan in the year 1970. In the mid 1970s, monk Wu Qian residing in India took up the post of first Abbot of the Chinese temple. He devoted over 10 years to plan the construction of the temple, the main hall, the monastic dining hall and building for the stay of believers of Buddhism. In the year 2009, master Rizhao came to India on pilgrimage and visited Bodhgaya. Then in 2011, master Rizhao was appointed Abbot of the Chinese temple. The Chinese Ambassador to India Mr. Le Yucheng visited the Chinese Buddha temple on 11th November 2015 and donated 200,000 RMB for the construction of the temple on behalf of the Chinese Government. The Monastery provides a comfortable stay to the people of China visiting Bodhgaya to get blessings from Buddha. A small office is maintained by Chinese people for the upkeep of the temple. Chinese officials maintain office records in Chinese and have very little knowledge of Hindi or English. Our discussion continued through a mobile application. A young lady visitor from China who was working for some Indian firm from Shanghai was well versed in English and acted as an interpreter to facilitate our talks with the Chinese Buddha temple officials.

Gate, Chinese Monastery

Statue of Lord Buddha in Chinese Temple

ROYAL BHUTAN MONASTERY

The Royal Bhutan Monastery is situated near the Indosan Nipponji temple. There are vibrant and colorful frescoes and paintings from the life of Buddha here.

ROYAL BHUTAN MONASTERY

Painting at Royal Bhutan Monastery

Gate, Buddha Temple

Statue of Buddha in Royal Bhutan Monastery

80 FEET BUDDHA

This towering 80 feet high statue of Buddha is an important monument at Bodhgaya, visible from far and wide. The construction of this statue was started in 1986 and was completed in September 1989.

This 80 feet high statue of lord Buddha was unveiled by His Holy Highness Dalai Lama in November 1989. The Japanese call it 'Daivutso' which means Great Buddha.

80 Feet Buddha (Daivutso)

Statues of Disciples of Buddha in Daivutsu Temple Complex

DAIJOKYO MONASTERY

In Japanese, 'Dai' means great and 'jokyo' means the wheel of law. A Japanese lady Sugigama, follower of the Nichren sect, was instrumental in the construction of this temple. A plot measuring two acres was allotted by the Government of Bihar. The then President of India, late Gyani Zail Singh, inaugurated this temple on 13th February 1983. The two storey temple building is built out of concrete in Japanese architecture. The temple affairs are looked after by a Secretary. The head office of this organization is in Nagoya, Japan.

Daijokyo Monastery (Japanese)

Statue of Sugiyama

INDOSAN NIPPONJI JAPANESE MONASTERY

Indosan Nipponji Japanese Monastery is situated on the road passing behind the Bangladesh monastery. This Japanese Temple was erected by the International Buddhist Brotherhood Association Kokusai Bukkkyo Koryu Kyokai in Bodhgaya in 1963 as the synthetic society of all Japanese sects and schools. The making of this temple is based on peace and an everlasting international reconciliation between human beings who have experienced successive world wars.

The International Buddhist Association is registered at the Ministry of Japan and its sister society, the International Buddhist Brotherhood Association of India was registered with the Government of Bihar in 1986 under the provisions of Societies Registration Act of 1860. The first project of International Buddhist Brotherhood Association in Bodhgaya was completed in February 1970, and the second step of this project was completed in November 1973.It was then formally inaugurated by the then President of India V. V. Giri in December 1973. As the third step, the construction of a kindergarten attached to this temple was completed in February 1977, and the school started functioning from September 15, 1977. At present, it teaches 208 children from the ages of 3 to 5 years. As the fourth step, a charitable clinic was established by All Japan Buddhist Women Association in 1984. It provides free medical services to the local people who need it.

The temple has been erected on a raised platform in Japanese architecture. The Buddha statue inside has been built in 'Abhaya Mudra'. The wall behind and on either side of the Buddha statue is decorated with a beautiful painting depicting a large gathering.

Indosan Nipponji Temple

Indosan Nipponji Temple

Image of Buddha and Painting Indosan Nipponji Temple

Indosan Nipponji Temple

TIBETAN MONASTERIES OF BODHGAYA

There are numerous monasteries erected by Buddhists from various sects followed in Tibet. To name an important one, there is the monastery of Gelupa of the Mahayana sect of Buddhism, situated about 100 meters to the west of Mahabodhi temple. It was erected in 1934 by Lama Khenpo Ngawang Samten.

Palyul Thubten Shedrub Monastery's construction was started in 1994 and came to its successful completion in September 2015. This monastery is situated at a distance of a few hundred meters from the Great Buddha statue. This monastery has been established as a branch of Namdroling Monastery, as per the intentions of H.H. Penor Rinpoche.

Karma Monastery is also a very attractive Tibetan monastery. The vibrant colours of the monastery attract the people of faith and tourists alike. It is situated next to the Japanese temple.

Another important Tibetan temple is the Treger monastery situated on the Bodhgaya-Gaya bypass road. It was established by Mingyur Rinpoche in the year 2007. This monastery serves a large number of people visiting Buddhist events. A school is also run by the monastery.

Shechen Tennyi Dargyeling monastery was established by Sheachen Rabjam Rinpoche, the spiritual heir and grandson of Dilago Kheyentse, in 1966. The temple walls here are decorated with frescoes on the life of Buddha, painted by the teachers and students from Tsering Art School. There is beautiful stupa within the monastery compound.

Karma Tibetan Temple

Treger Monastery

Treger Monastery

Shechen Monastery

Archaeological Survey o
established a museum i
the year 1956. It is a fe
away from the Mahabod
museum consists of two
open courtyard. The mu
bronze and stone sculp
and Brahminical faith o

Stupa in Palyul Monastery

DHUNGESHWARI OR PRAGBODHI

About 15 kms from Bodhgaya are some hillocks. There is a small cave in one of these hillocks where Buddha is said to have lived before reaching Bodhgaya. In the Buddhist scriptures, the place is mentioned as Prag Bodhi – a place prior to enlightenment.

A statue of Buddha depicting his body in skeleton has been placed inside the cave. A stupa has also been erected here. A bird's eye view of the valley can be had from the top of this hill.

Dungeshwari Hills

Statue of Lord Buddha Dungeshwari Cave

Stupa at Dungeshwari hill

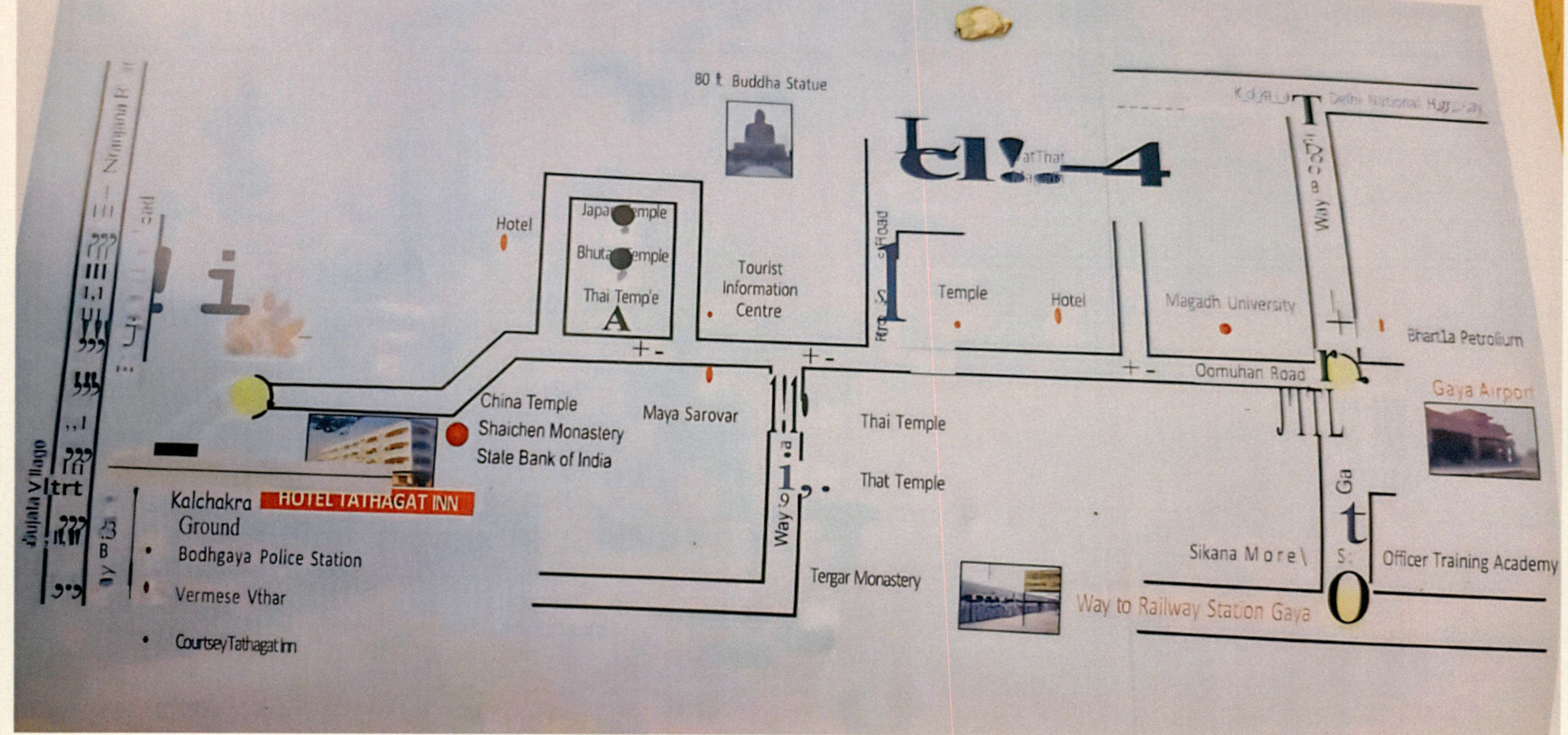
80 ft Buddha Statue
Hotel
Thai Temple
Tourist Information Centre
Temple
Hotel
Magadh University
Bhartia Petrolium
Gaya Airport
Oomuhan Road
China Temple
Shaichen Monastery
Stale Bank of India
Maya Sarovar
Thai Temple
That Temple
Tergar Monastery
Sikana More
Officer Training Academy
Way to Railway Station Gaya
HOTEL TATHAGAT INN
Kalchakra Ground
Bodhgaya Police Station
Vermese Vthar
Courtsey Tathagat Inn
Sujata Village

Biblography

1. Buddha Philosophy, Rahul Sankrantyana, Kitab Mahal Allahabad, 1943.
2. The Wonder that was India, by A.L. Basham, 1954.
3. Cultural Glimpses of Buddhist Literature, Parashu Ram Chaturvedi, 1958.
4. History of Development of Buddhism, Dr. Govind Chandra Pandey, 1963.
5. History of Buddhism in India, Lama Tara Nath, Patana, 1971.
6. Buddhist Monuments, D. Mitra, Calcutta, 1971.
7. The Heart of Buddhist Meditation Rider and Company London-1975.
8. The Buddhistic Remains of Bihar, A.M. Broadley, Bharti Prakashan.
9. Sarnath, V.S. Agarwal, Archeological Survey of India, 1984.
10. Pali Language and Literature Indra Chandra Shastri, Delhi University, 1987.
11. Buddhist Shrines, Dr. D.C. Bhattacharya, Publication Division, Govt. of India 1987.
12. Buddha Period Geography of India, Dr. Bharat Singh Upadhaya Allahabad, 1991.

13. Buddha His Life, His doctrine, His Order Dr. Herman Oldenberg, Lancer International-1992.

14. Buddhist Sacred Places of India, Prof. Sangh Sen Singh, Publication Division Govt. of India 1994.

15. Buddha, Dipak Chopra, Harper Collins-2007.

16. Encyclopedia of Buddhism, D.N. Chaddha, Max Ford Books, New Delhi-2008.

17. Dharma Chakra Maha Bodhi Society of India 2014.

18. Dharmadoot Maha Bodhi Society of India 2016.

List of the Important Places of Interest in Bodhgaya

1. Mahabodhi Mahavir (Main Temple)
2. Tibetan Temple
3. Jay Sri Mahabodhi Temple
4. Shechen Temple
5. Chinese Temple
6. Museum
7. Tamang Temple
8. Bangladesh Temple
9. Royal Thai Temple
10. Royal Bhutan Temple
11. Japan Temple (Nipponji)
12. Japan Temple (Daijokyo)
13. 80 Feet Buddha Statue
14. Palyul Namdroling Temple
15. Vajra Kilaya Temple
16. Karma Temple
17. All India Bhikku Sangh
18. Nyingma Monlam Monastery
19. Druck Ngawang Thupten Choeling

20. Tergar Monastery
21. Burmese Vihar
22. Sujata Girah
23. Suja Kheer Offering Temple
24. Dhamaran
25. Lodruk Kawa University
26. Dugeshwari (Pladen Shawa Drakphok)
27. Kuleshwari (Jigsu Rungwai Durtoe)
28. Watpa Buddhist Bharat Society (Wanawas Place)